5

Best Ways

to Amuse Kids

51 Best Ways to Amuse Kids

Ellen van Wees

A Perigee Book

A Perigee Book
Published by The Berkley Publishing Group
A division of Penguin Putnam Inc.
375 Hudson Street
New York, New York 10014

Copyright © 2000 by Ellen van Wees
Book design by Tiffany Kukec
Cover art and design by Miguel Santana

First edition: June 2000

Published simultaneously in Canada.

The Penguin Putnam Inc. World Wide Web site address is
http://www.penguinputnam.com

Library of Congress Cataloging-in-Publication Data

Van Wees, Ellen.
    51 best ways to amuse kids / Ellen van Wees.
        p. cm.
    ISBN 0-399-52607-2
        1. Amusements. 2. Play. I. Title: Fifty-one best ways to amuse kids. II. Title.

GV1201 .V35 2000
790.1'922—dc21   00-026697

Printed in the United States of America

10   9   8   7   6   5   4   3   2   1

This book is dedicated to my parents,
Cathy and Adam Mientjes.

Acknowledgments

Many thanks go to my agent, Ling Lucas, for her warm encouragement and to my editor, Sheila Curry, for her insightful suggestions. Also, thanks go out to family and friends who shared great stories and helpful tips.

Contents

Activity Key

Indoor 🏠

Outdoor 🌳🌷🌼

Travel 🛒

Introduction

From my many years as a children's party entertainer, I have picked the 51 best ideas to amuse kids. Whether it be for a birthday party, or while traveling, standing in line at the grocery store, or spending time at home, this selection is a rescue kit for when you're at a loss for ideas and need one right away.

This easy-access book is designed to open up at any page. Each activity comes with a quick guide to indicate whether it's for indoors, outdoors, or travel, for which age group and how many players are recommended. It also provides information on what supplies you will need for each activity.

Some activities are short and will tide you over for a few minutes to an hour. Others will keep kids busy for hours, sometimes days. The range of activities will appeal to different skill levels; some are educational, some are relaxing, and some are just plain silly fun. Some of them require adult supervision because they involve using sharp tools or the oven.

Many of these games may inspire you and the child to think up your own ideas, and all offer opportunities for bonding and developing important play skills.

#1 Balloon Float

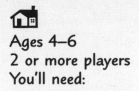

Ages 4–6
2 or more players
You'll need:

- 1 balloon per child
- approximately 5 yards of open space for the race

Kids love the excitement of not letting the balloons touch the ground. This is a slow and gentle race. **Be sure that children don't chew or swallow balloons; they can be a choking hazard.**

1. Blow up different colored balloons, one for each person.

2. Decide on a finish line at least 5 yards from the start line.

3. Have kids blow their balloons across the room to the finish line without letting them touch the floor. They can also

"bump" the balloons along with their heads. There is only one rule: no hands allowed.

If there's 1 child in the game, join in! But let her cross the finish line first.

#2 Leprechauns and Giants

Ages 3–6
Best with 2 or more players
You'll need:

- a tape or CD player
- tapes/CDs of favorite children's songs; any of the *Sesame Street* collections are great

This game gives kids a sense of how much space their bodies take up in different positions. It's especially good for young kids who are learning the concepts of "small" and "big."

1. Play a popular kids' tape or CD during this game.

2. The chosen leader (each child gets a turn) yells "giants!" and everyone grows as big as they can, stretching their bodies tall.

3. The leader yells "leprechauns!" and everyone shrinks as small as they can.

4. When the music stops, everyone must freeze.

    This is loads of fun. There will be a lot of laughing and giggling, and freezing is generally impossible under these circumstances.

#3 Ahoy, Ye Landlubbers!

Ages 4 and up
2–3 players
You'll need:

- sheets of newspaper, 1 per child
- plastic margarine containers or the bottom thirds of plastic soda bottles (which an adult can cut off with scissors), 1 per child
- construction paper or cardboard
- adhesive tape
- plastic straws
- pieces of colored ribbon
- coins wrapped in aluminum foil
- clean pebbles or small bars of soap

This project culminates with all the kids packed into the tub for a fun bath time or, on a summer's day, in a kiddie pool. Start the game with the making of pirate hats (see page

9), which everyone wears while making the pirate boats (see page 10). After the kids settle into the tub or pool, the real fun begins. You can tell them pirate adventures and stories or act out stories of your own.

> For further enjoyment, read some great pirate stories together. *Treasure Island* by Robert Louis Stevenson, for example, is a great adventure tale. Or read about the lives of real pirates, such as Blackbeard, Calico Jack, and Captain Kidd. Don't forget the two infamous female pirates, Anne Bonny and Mary Read.

1. The adult is the stranded landlubber. You hold the treasure (coins wrapped in aluminum foil) in a plastic container, and the cutthroat pirates threaten you with their (imaginary) cutlasses: "Surrender your treasure or we'll cut you to pieces!" They steal your treasure and load it onto their boats.

2. At sea the pirates attempt to take each other's treasure. They threaten to keelhaul their enemies or make them walk the plank! They can sink each other's ships by filling them with clean pebbles or small bars of soap.

Instructions for Making a Pirate Hat

1. Take a full sheet of newspaper, large-format or tabloid size, and fold along the existing crease.

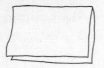

2. Turn down the corners of the folded edge of newspaper to the center.

3. Fold up the bottom edge of newspaper and crease the fold. Turn the paper over and do the same on the other side.

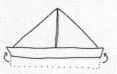

4. Open up the hat and place it on the child's head.

Instructions for Making a Pirate Boat

1. Use an empty margarine container or the bottom third of a plastic soda bottle.

2. Cut out a triangle for the sail from construction paper or cardboard; tape it to a plastic straw, and then tape the "mast" to the inside of container.

3. Make a Jolly Roger flag by cutting out a smaller triangle from paper and drawing a skull and crossbones on it. Attach it to the top of the "mast" and add colored ribbons above it. Now "she's true and yare!"

#4 Caution!! Kids Working
(or Who Goes There? Friend or Foe?)

Ages 3–6
Best with 2 or more players
You'll need:

- the use of the living room or den
- sofa cushions
- sheets and/or tablecloths
- a broom
- armchairs or kitchen chairs
- a flashlight
- some scary books to read (see box)

Remember the joy of building your own fort in the living room with sofa cushions, chairs, and sheets? Part of the fun was having momentary control over the "grown-up room" and creating a house within a house. Here's how you can re-create this magic for kids.

1. Make a secret hideaway by taking sofa cushions and standing them up like a wall a few feet away from the couch. Place sheets (or tablecloths) over the top to create a roof. Add a sheet at each end for a door.

> Books to read inside the hideout can include *The Legend of Sleepy Hollow* by Washington Irving, *A Woggle of Witches* by Adrienne Adams, and *Nightmares or Poems to Trouble Your Sleep* by Jack Prelutsky.

2. Make a tented structure by standing a broom between cushions and placing a large sheet over it. Tuck the corners of the sheet under chairs, placed in a circle around the broom.

3. Figure out a secret password so that no strangers can be admitted. Feel free to change the password from time to time.

Another fun thing to do is to turn the lights down in the room, bring a flashlight inside the fort, and take turns telling spooky stories.

#5 Finger Doodles

Ages 5 and older
1 child at a time, and one adult
No supplies necessary

This is an excellent traveling game. It's also good for calming a child before bedtime.

1. Use a finger to trace a letter on the child's back and have him guess what it is. Help him along by giving clues. For example, for the letter "a," tell him it's the first letter in the word "apple."

2. Between each letter, rub his back as if erasing the letter from a blackboard. This makes the guessing game easier for him and gives you an opportunity to soothe him with a nice rub.

3. Continue with different letters; eventually, you can trace out his name.

4. You can also draw a face and have the child guess the parts of the face.

As you can imagine, this game easily turns into a soothing back rub session or a fun tickling game!

#6 Nature Calls

Ages 4–10
Best with 2 or more players
You'll need:

- a plastic sandwich bag
- a glass or plastic jar with a lid with holes punched in it
- a magnifying glass (if you have one)

There is nothing like a nice little wander through a park, a forest, a lovely meadow, or the seaside, letting the smell of grass, leaves, or salty air open up the senses. If you bring along a sandwich bag and a jar with a lid with air holes, you will be all set for an interesting time. Remind children to collect only things that have already fallen from a tree or plant, so that they don't damage living things.

A nature corner can be set
up anywhere in the home; it
is best at the child's height.
It can be a small shelf or a
special small table where all
the objects can be lined up,
rearranged, and studied.

As you stroll under the canopy of trees or across a field:

1. Ask the kids to collect nature's treasures. These can be leaves, bugs, stones, bark, shells, etc. Live bugs or snails can go in the jar . . . until it's time to free them. (Let the kids decide when, and remind them that the creatures live longer in their own environment.) These treasures can be exhibited in a "nature corner" in their room at home.

2. Ask kids to:
   - pay attention to smells
   - listen for sounds
   - experience different textures of leaves, stones, bark, etc.
   - take turns discovering items and pointing them out to you

3. Play hide-and-seek.

4. Have the kids search the sky for cloud pictures. Tell them about the people from the island of Singatree, who believe that clouds take the shape of the most prevalent thing on

the ground in the area. For example, if there are lots of rabbits hopping on the ground, there will be cloud rabbits; if there is a windmill in the area, chances are there will be one in the sky, too.

#7 Bang on a Can

Ages 4 and up
Best with at least 4 kids
You'll need:

- a variety of kitchen utensils (described below)
- tape player and blank tape (optional)

The fun begins when you start to gather your musical instruments.

1. From the kitchen gather as many sturdy objects as possible, objects that can take a mild beating. Perhaps you'll have to search in the garage, too. Look for surfaces and materials that make interesting sounds—wooden spoons, ladles, chopsticks, old pots and pans, lids, colanders, graters, etc. all make great percussion instruments.

2. Fill coffee cans or soda bottles partially with rice or beans and cover them with lids. Now you have some cool maracas.

3. Plastic bottles, filled with varying levels of water, are great as wind instruments when you blow over the tops of them.

With all the instruments ready, you have a wonderful orchestra:

1. Try to get loud sounds and soft sounds. If the band creates a rhythm or a pattern, stick with it for a while, then mix it up. Cacophonous as it may be, it will be a joyful, irreverent mix of new sounds.

2. Have each child choose his favorite instrument. Get into a circle and look at each other while playing the instrument of choice.

3. Compose a "symphony" together.

4. If you can, tape the "symphony" and play it back. This is guaranteed to put a grin on everyone's face.

#8 It's a Puppet Show!!!!!

Ages 4 and up
Best with 3 or more players
You'll need:

- puppets (you may already have some, but it's fun and easy to make your own)
- old socks
- markers
- Sobo or heavy white craft glue
- assorted buttons
- colored felt pieces
- yarn
- paper plates
- Popsicle sticks

This is an activity that can be an hour of fun or inspire days of lasting enjoyment. There are two ways to use the puppets. For free play, let the kids' imaginations run the show. If you want to get children involved in giving a performance, then, *before* you start making the puppets, get them thinking about a story for the show. The hero and heroine of the story could be their family pet, relatives, schoolmates, or their favorite toys. You could also perform such perennial favorites as *Peter Pan*, *Cinderella*, or *The Three Little Pigs*. They will create puppets to match the story they want to tell.

You will have fun rehearsing a couple of times. When they feel comfortable enough to perform the show for others, invite an audience. You can even make tickets to hand out for the show.

1. If you don't have any puppets, it's no problem. They're easy to make, and creating your own is fun. Make them from old socks, as long as they're clean and have no holes. With markers, draw faces on the socks. You can also glue parts of the face onto the sock, such as buttons for eyes, felt for a nose and mouth, and yarn for hair.

      Or
   Another quick, easy way to make a puppet is to tape a Popsicle stick to the back of a paper plate. Draw a face on the front, and add yarn for hair.

2. Make an instant theater by taping up a sheet in a doorway, just high enough to allow kids to comfortably hold puppets above the edge of the sheet.

Or

Place a cloth big enough to cover the front and top of a table and have kids do the show behind it. Players kneel behind table facing audience and perform show with puppets above table edge.

Kids can really get into the process of creating a show. The more they're involved in making the puppets and conceiving the story, the more satisfied and excited they'll be.

#9 Dressing Game

🏠

Ages 3–4
Best with 1 player
You'll need:

- clothes in your wardrobe

Children who are learning how to dress themselves are proud to show they can do this by themselves.

1. Pretend you're going on an outing or to work. Put clothing items on wrong or on the wrong parts of your body. For example, put on a shirt or blouse back to front or trousers on your arms, shoes on your hands, or a jacket on your head.

2. Walk to the door as if to leave dressed like that, then say to the child, "I'm ready!"

3. Watch the surprise on her face when she sees that you've got it all mixed up! Feigning concern, you can say, "What's wrong?" She will certainly straighten you out. You can encourage her to be specific about what isn't right. For

example, "How should my shirt be put on?" or "Where should my shoes go?"

This game's a real child-pleaser because it places the child in control. The child can take charge and tell you how to put clothes on properly.

#10 My Favorite Book

🏠

Ages 2–5
1–2 players
You'll need:

- corrugated cardboard box
- poster board or cardboard cereal box
- a selection of magazines, catalogs, etc. from which child can cut pictures
- photographs of the child doing an activity, or from holidays, birthdays, etc.
- adult and child-safe scissors
- hole punch
- 1½ yards of brightly colored ribbon or yarn (that child has chosen) cut into 3 pieces of equal length
- glue stick

Making a book with a child's favorite pictures or photos is a beautiful way to create a tangible childhood memory that you can store for safekeeping until the child grows up. It's also a lovely way to spend a rainy day or quiet evening with a child.

1. From a corrugated cardboard box, cut 2 squares or rectangles for the outside cover of the book. A good size is 8 inches square or 8 inches x 6 inches. Set these aside.

2. Next, on the poster board or cereal box cardboard use a ruler to trace up to 10 same-size pages. You'll need to make the pages slightly smaller (⅛ inch) than the cover. Allow an older child to carefully cut out the pieces; if the child is younger, you will need to do the cutting. If you cut out 10 pieces, this will give you 20 pages.

3. Leaving a ¾-inch margin from the left edge of each cardboard piece, measure 3 evenly spaced places to punch holes for binding. Give the child a pencil and show him where he can mark places for 3 holes.

4. With a hole punch, punch holes at the marked places.

5. Now the child picks out the pictures to put on the pages. Younger children are happy to put in randomly chosen pictures. You may want to encourage older children to have a theme or narrative for their book. For example, he may want a nature theme and have photographs of all kinds of animals. He can include pictures of himself at the zoo. Or he may want to tell a story about the neighborhood he lives in or a vacation he has taken by choosing pictures of a plane flying or a car driving through the countryside. A picture

of a house at the end of the book could show the return home.

6. After the pictures are selected, help him glue the backs of the pictures with the glue stick and place them carefully on the pages. It's fine to leave empty pages so there'll be opportunities to add pictures later.

7. When the glue has dried on the pages, place one piece of the corrugated cardboard (back cover) on the table, followed by the 10 poster board pieces; then place the second corrugated piece (front cover) on top. Make sure all the pages are lined up neatly.

8. The child takes a piece of ribbon or yarn and threads it through the top hole of the top cover, the pages, and the bottom cover (you may need to assist). Tie a bow or double knot, snugly but not too tight. Do the same for the other two holes. Test the pages to make sure they open easily; if they don't, adjust the knot.

9. Help the child come up with a book title. Write it on the front cover. Don't forget the author's name.

10. After you've helped him clean up, you can sit together and go through the book. Encourage him to talk about each

page by asking questions such as "What's this one?" "Why do you like this picture?" "Where's this giraffe going?" "What does it eat?" and "Where does it sleep?" At the end of making this book, you'll have one satisfied author!

#11 Gimme Five

Ages 3 and up
Any number of players
You'll need:

- newspapers to protect the floor or other surface you are working on
- construction paper or heavy white paper
- nontoxic tempera or kids' craft paint in several colors
- old kitchen dinner plates (or plastic plates)
- child-safe scissors
- markers
- smocks, or clothing that can get paint and markers on it

This is a good craft project for a rainy day. Kids will love making "hand" greeting cards.

1. Make sure children are properly smocked or wearing their "paint" clothes.

You don't have to spend money on a smock to protect your child's clothes when doing craft projects. An old button-down-the-front shirt from any adult will do. The child wears the shirt backward, protecting his clothes. You can cut the sleeves to fit the child.

2. Cover table or floor area with newspapers and lay out sheets of construction or heavy white paper on top. Pour different colors of paint onto plates.

3. Child places flat hand, fingers splayed, onto plate of paint, covering entire surface of hand (you may need to assist younger children).

4. She then places her hand flat on the paper. Help her press down firmly and help her lift her hand in one single move. She will have a beautiful handprint.

5. When the paint is dry, the handprint can be cut out and a greeting written on the back by the child.

6. After the big cleanup you can play a hand game with the younger kids (see next activity).

#12 Open Shut Them!

Ages 3–5
At least 1 player
No supplies necessary

This simple hand game can be played anywhere.

1. Sit facing the child and act out the words to this song. For example, open your hands wide and then crunch them into fists. For the line "lap, lap, lap," slap your lap three times. On "Do not let them in!" quickly hide your hands behind your back.

The song goes like this:

> Open shut them, open shut them,
> Give a little clap, clap, clap
> Open shut them, open shut them,
> Lay them in your lap, lap, lap

Creep them, creep them, creep them, creep them,
Right up to your chin, chin, chin,
Open wide your little mouth,
Do not let them in!

#13 Mauve, Melon, Marmoset (Categories)

Ages 6–10
2 or more players
You'll need:

- pen and paper if indoors
- a good memory if outdoors or traveling

This game will eat up the time while you're waiting in line or driving on a trip.

1. Think up 3 different categories, such as country, fruit, and color.

2. Pick a letter, such as "B," and say or write down an example of each category beginning with that letter. For instance: Brazil, banana, and blue.

3. Give each player 2 minutes to complete all categories. The first to complete, wins. If you don't use pencil and paper, you can shout out the answers.

4. You can keep the same categories or think up new ones. And if it gets too easy, shorten the time limit.

#14 Luminarias

Ages 6–10
More fun with 2 or more players
You'll need:

- 6 white or brown lunch bags
- pencil
- child-safe scissors
- 6 tea (or votive) candles
- matches
- sand or pebbles

Paper lanterns lit with candles are used to welcome Baby Jesus on Christmas Eve in Spanish-speaking areas. These lanterns, called luminarias, are made from paper bags that have designs cut in them to let the candlelight shine through. You can adapt this tradition for any time of the year and for any occasion. For example, you could cut out a pumpkin face for Halloween or a child's name for a birthday. (Candles and matches should *always* be handled carefully, under adult supervision.)

1. Take a bag and fold it in half. Draw a simple design on the bag (see illustration).

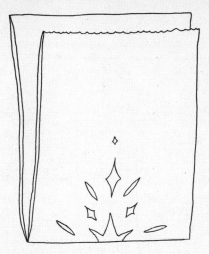

2. Cut out the design, cutting through all 4 layers of the bag (assist younger children).

3. Open the bag and place a layer of sand or pebbles at the bottom; set the candle in the middle of the bottom.

4. When it's dark, place the luminarias outside, lining a pathway to the door. You can light the candles with a long match

or pick up the candle and light it, then carefully place it back in the bag. You can use a luminaria to decorate a table indoors as well.

#15 Rock Pools

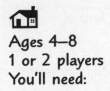

Ages 4–8
1 or 2 players
You'll need:

- a selection of rocks found on excursions or bought at a garden store
- a large, low basin or tray (1–2 feet in diameter)
- tap water

Children are fascinated with rocks: holding them, feeling the different textures, and looking at them. The colors of the rocks become intense when they are submerged in water. Kids will enjoy making these beautiful rock pools. If you're in the mood for a field trip, a good book to bring along is *The Field Guide to Rocks and Minerals* by Frederick Pough (Houghton Mifflin).

1. Wash any loose dirt from the rocks.

2. Place rocks touching each other in the basin.

3. Pour water over the rocks so that they are completely submerged.

4. To bring out the colors more, use a light-colored basin or place a white cloth under the rocks.

5. Place the rock pool where it won't be knocked over and where child can reach it easily.

#16 Balloon Madness

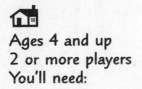

Ages 4 and up
2 or more players
You'll need:

- balloons for each child
- good strong lungs

Who can resist the silly, irreverent sounds that come with letting air out of balloons, or resist letting them rocket off into the air and see them fly around the room? We've all done this. It's fun for all ages. **Watch that children don't chew on balloons; they can be a choking hazard.**

1. Let the kids blow up balloons as big as they can. Get them to help younger kids with theirs.

2. Using both hands, slowly release air from balloon by stretching the opening with the forefingers and thumbs; a screeching sound will occur. You can vary the pitch by stretching the opening to different lengths.

3. Release the balloon and watch it take its random trajectory through space.

4. Let kids repeat this process until you can't stand it anymore!

#17 Story Time Switch

Ages 4–8
Best with 1 player
No supplies necessary

Here's a great way to develop a child's imagination. Instead of you telling the child a story, switch roles and have the child tell you a story. You'll be amazed and entertained at the twists and turns of storytelling he will take you through. This is a superb game to do while waiting in line or at a doctor's office, or while traveling.

Here are some ways to get him started. Say you would like him to tell you a story. If he doesn't dive in right away, you can help him along:

- Start him off with "Once upon a time . . ."
- Ask him questions about the characters or events or places he is describing (e.g., What color was the dragon? How big was he? Where did he live?)
- Another good question is "What happened next?"

Because this invented story could turn out to be never-ending, you can say "I really liked hearing your story. Let's stop it for now, and continue it next time (or at bedtime)."

#18 Threading Necklaces

Ages 4–8
1–4 players
You'll need:

- plastic cord in a variety of colors (can be found at a craft store)
- a selection of plastic, wood, or clay beads
- plain or colored pasta with holes (penne, macaroni, etc.)
- scissors

Both girls and boys love this project. Kids make their own necklaces with easy-to-thread plastic cord and beads or pasta. This is a wonderful activity for developing children's motor skills.

1. Help child measure the necklace length, making it long enough to put it over his head and take it off without untying the knot.

2. Let the child select the beads he would like and line them up in sequence for threading.

3. The child ties a knot at one end and threads the necklace.

4. Once the beads are strung, tie the ends of the necklace together. Now everyone has a beautiful ready-to-wear accessory.

#19 Grandmother's Trunk

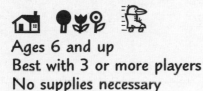

Ages 6 and up
Best with 3 or more players
No supplies necessary

This is a great memory game for a party, traveling or waiting in line.

1. Children sit in a circle on the floor. The first child begins by saying, "My grandmother has an old trunk. And in her trunk are apples."

2. The next child repeats the first sentence and adds to the second an item that begins with the next letter of the alphabet, such as "And in her trunk are apples and bunnies."

3. The following child repeats everything said by the previous player plus another item beginning with the next letter of the alphabet; in this case, it could be cars. And so on.

4. The game continues all the way through the alphabet. All players must remember everything in order.

#20 I Heard It Through the Grapevine

🏠 🏓🌷🌱

Ages 6–8
4 or more children
No supplies necessary

This is a great party or indoor rainy day game. Sometimes called "telephone," it shows us how easy it is to misunderstand each other! It is also lots of laughs.

1. Players sit in a circle close to each other.

2. The first child thinks up a sentence and whispers it into the ear of the child to his left, who whispers it to the next child, and so on until it has gone around the circle.

3. The last child says the sentence out loud as he heard it. It's surprising and funny to hear how different it is from the original sentence!

4. The second child makes up a sentence and passes it on. This continues until everyone has had a turn to say the sentence first.

A great alternative to this game is Pass the Face, in which one person makes a silly face, shows it to the group in the circle, and then passes the face to the next person. The fun comes from seeing so many silly variations of the funny face. Giggles galore!

#21 Tickle Me!

Ages 4 and up
2 players
No supplies necessary

A ticklish game that's fun while traveling or simply just because. . . .

1. Ask the child to extend her bare arm toward you. She must guess when she feels your fingers on the inside crease of her arm.

2. Say "I'm going to creep my fingers from your hand all the way to here," and touch the inside crease of her arm. "When I get to here, you have to say 'stop.' " The child must keep her eyes shut the whole time, no peeking. Usually the child guesses far short of the designated goal.

3. After a few tries, you can switch and have her do the same to you.

It's the rare child who can play this game without giggling.

#22 Peas Porridge Hot

Ages 4–6
2 or 4 players
No supplies necessary

This is a great waiting game that is played with hands and a rhyme.

1. Players face each other, clap hands, and say the rhyme below.

2. The clapping sequence goes like this: They clap their own hands together, then right hands together, then left hands together, then their own hands together again, and so on, in time with the rhythm of the poem.

3. The goal is to clap and chant faster and faster until they can't stand the excitement anymore and keel over laughing.

> Peas porridge hot,
> Peas porridge cold,
> Peas porridge in the pot,
> Nine days old.

Some like it hot,
Some like it cold,
Some like it in the pot,
Nine days old.

#23 Wait a Minute!

Ages 4 or older (old enough to understand time)
Best with 1 child
You'll need:

- a watch or clock with a sweep second hand or a stop-watch

Ask the child how long a minute feels like. You'll find that this game will get you wondering, too, and you'll both have fun guessing.

1. Have child turn his back to the clock or close his eyes. Then say, "Now." The child guesses when a minute is up. When he says "Stop," click the stopwatch or show him where the second hand was on the clock when he said "Stop." Keep trying until he can guess when the hand is within 5 seconds, either way, of a minute.

2. Switch now, and have him look at the clock while you try to guess when a minute has passed. This is not easy to do.

When he is allowed to watch the clock, he gets a different sense of time.

#24 Spoon Puppets

🏠

Ages 6–10
2–6 players
You'll need:

- 1 wooden spoon per child
- poster paint
- paintbrushes
- glue
- scraps of fabric and lace
- yarn, feathers, tinsel for hair
- markers
- smocks or old shirts to protect clothes
- newspapers to protect the work area

Did you know that wooden spoons are really characters in disguise? Kids know this. That's why they love to reveal the spoons' true identities by dressing them up and turning them into puppets.

1. Spread newspaper or an old tablecloth on a table.

2. Paint a wooden spoon a background color: a flesh tone or blue or orange or whatever the child wishes. Let it dry.

3. While the spoon is drying, choose "hair" for the puppet: yarn, tinsel, or feathers. Also, decide what kind of costume to dress the puppet in by choosing from scraps of fabric and lace. Arrange the pieces on the table.

4. When the spoon is dry, draw the facial features on the bowl of the spoon with paint or markers.

5. Glue the "hair" on the top and the back of the bowl.

4. Glue the costume to the handle.

5. To stand the puppet upright, you can set it in a ball of clay or plasticine, or in a clear glass bottle.

6. If you make several puppets, you can have an impromptu puppet show. (See #8, "It's a Puppet Show!!!!!," for puppet show ideas.) Just make sure the dish doesn't run away with your spoon!

#25 Scissors, Rock, Paper

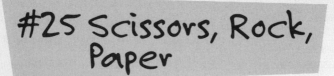

Ages 4–6
2–3 children
No supplies necessary

This is a very old game in which there's no real winning or losing. It's more a game of chance, and kids love the repetition. It can also be used in deciding who goes first in any other game.

1. All players hide a hand behind their backs. They choose one of three different gestures that represent different symbols. SCISSORS: The index and middle fingers make a "V." ROCK: Make a fist. PAPER: Hand opens flat, palm down.

2. At the count of 3, players show their hands.

3. Kids say out loud what the gestures represent:
   • Rock crushes scissors but is covered by paper.
   • Paper covers rock but is cut by scissors.
   • Scissors cut paper but is crushed by rock.

#26 The Lady with the Alligator Purse

Ages 4–6
2 players
No supplies necessary

This a super hand-clapping game. It becomes fast and furious, and you end up feeling sorry for the poor little turtle!

1. Two kids face each other and chant the following rhyme (which they'll memorize quickly) while alternating clapping their own hands, right hands, left hands, their own hands, their laps, and their own hands again, repeating this throughout the rhyme.

2. The rhythm builds slowly and goes faster and faster until they've reached lightning speed at the end. Older kids will soon develop intricate clapping variations on their own.

> Miss Lucy had a turtle,
> His name was Tiny Tim.

She put him in the bathtub
To teach him how to swim.

He drank up all the water,
He ate up all the soap,
He tried to eat the bathtub,
But it wouldn't go down his throat.

Miss Lucy called the doctor,
Miss Lucy called the nurse,
Miss Lucy called the Lady
with the Alligator Purse.

"Mumps," said the doctor,
"Measles," said the nurse,
"Nothing," said the Lady
with the Alligator Purse.

Out walked the doctor,
Out walked the nurse,
Out walked the Lady
with the Alligator Purse.

#27 A String of Paper Dolls

Ages 4–8
2–6 players
You'll need:

- sheets of white or colored paper
  (8½ x 11 inches)
- scissors
- pencil
- markers
- glitter glue

This is a very old paper craft idea that hasn't lost its charm. At the end you'll have a lovely string of dolls that can decorate a window, a room, or a shelf.

1. Fold the paper widthwise into fourths, just like a concertina. Crease folds firmly.

2. Holding the folded paper, cut it in half so you'll have two pieces, each 4¼ x 5½ inches.

3. With the pencil draw a figure on *the top fold* of the paper (see illustration), making sure the drawing touches both sides of the fold.

4. Carefully cut out the figure through all *four folds*, being sure not to cut through folded edges.

5. Open up the string of dolls and fill in features, such as hair, face, and clothes. Accent with glitter if you like.

6. To make a long garland of dolls, make several of these rows and tape them together at the joints (hands, dress, or feet).

Hang the dolls across a window or above a bed. Instead of dolls, you can cut out flowers, stars, snowflakes, or animals.

#28 Banana Chocorama

Ages 4 and up
1–4 players
You'll need:

- peeled bananas (at least 1 for each child)
- bottle of chocolate syrup
- heavy plastic wrap or waxed paper
- small cookie sheet or large plate

These healthy frozen desserts are fun to make and are TOO yummy! Have kids take part in every step from peeling bananas to cleanup. While the bananas are freezing, and while the kids are in the kitchen, you can make "Valentines for Lunch" (activity #35).

1. Cover plate or cookie sheet with plastic wrap or waxed paper.

2. Pour chocolate syrup in a bowl.

3. Dip each banana into the syrup, coating half of it.

4. Arrange the bananas on the plate or cookie sheet so that they don't touch each other.

5. Place bananas in the freezer for at least 3 hours.

6. When serving them, wrap a napkin around the base of the banana without the chocolate.

#29 Think Globally

Ages 8 and up
2–6 players
No supplies necessary

Put on your thinking caps for this fabulous traveling game.

1. One person picks the name of a continent, country, city, town, state, or river, anywhere in the world, such as Wagga Wagga (Australia).

2. The next person must choose a name beginning with the last letter of the previous name, in this case "a." For example, Abu Dhabi (United Arab Emirates).

3. The next person may choose Iowa City (U.S.); the next, Yucatan (Mexico); and so on. Before you know it, you've been around the world a few times and you won't be hearing "Are we there yet?"

#30 Treasure Hunt

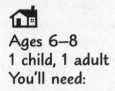

Ages 6–8
1 child, 1 adult
You'll need:

- paper
- markers or bright colored pens
- treats or treasure (see pages 66–67)

This is a great 1-child game. It also ensures that she gets the treasure every time! You'll need about 20 minutes of preparation time before you start the game, to write and hide clues for the child.

This game helps develop kids' language skills and is fun to boot. Keep the game short for younger kids; add more clues for older kids with more patience. At this age they're proud of their reading skills, so be sure to praise them as they read each clue. Here are some ideas for setting up clues.

1. Clues are written on pieces of paper and hidden in easy-to-find places. On the first piece of paper write WELCOME TO

THE (your family name) TREASURE HUNT. LOOK ON YOUR BED FOR THE FIRST CLUE!

2. For the first clue, write CLUE #1—LOOK UNDER THE CHAIR IN THE LIVING ROOM. Fold the paper in half, then in half again, and place it on the child's pillow. (You can fill in specifics about furniture or rooms in the house, e.g., Look under the blue chair or Look under dad's desk.)

3. For the second clue, write CLUE #2—LOOK INSIDE THE LAUNDRY BASKET. Fold this up and place it under the chair.

4. For the third clue, write CLUE #3—GO LOOK INSIDE THE COOKIE JAR ON THE KITCHEN COUNTER. Fold this up and place it inside the laundry basket.

5. Inside the cookie jar put a special treat wrapped up with the final note that says CONGRATULATIONS! YOU FOUND ME! Treats don't have to be sweets or cookies. See below for other treasure ideas.

Theme treasure hunts are fun, too. For example:

NATURE—the treasure could be an assortment of pretty seashells or an ant farm
DINOSAURS—dinosaur stickers

GANGSTERS AND DETECTIVES—a pair of
sunglasses
PIRATES—an eye patch and hat from a dime store
ASTRONOMY—a set of glow-in-the-dark planets and
stars

#31 Haunted House

Ages 4 and up
4 or more players, the more the merrier
You'll need:

- spare sheets and furniture
- a medium-size cardboard box (2 feet square)
- 1 pound cooked spaghetti
- 1 pound peeled grapes (large)
- 2 tablespoons vegetable oil
- large bowl
- stiff cardboard or construction paper to make "tickets"

This is an obvious game for Halloween, but it can be played any other time there is a call for something dark and spooky. Children can help prepare the spaghetti under adult supervision.

1. Kids build a makeshift "house" in a bedroom or living room,

using sheets stretched between sofas or between a dresser and bed.

2. For a scary "brain box," place the spaghetti, grapes, and oil in the large bowl and mix well. These are the "brains."

3. Place the box over the bowl of "brains" and cut holes that the kids will put their arms through so that they can feel the "brains" in the bowl. They won't be able to see what's in the bowl.

4. Place the covered bowl of "brains" inside the Haunted House, on the floor.

5. Kids make tickets for the invited guests and can charge admission. Darken the house so that they cannot see the box.

6. Each guest is invited to put their arms through the holes of the box and feel the "brains." An usher may need to guide them to the box.

7. Play Halloween music (found in the sound effects section in a music store) in the background to cover up the squeals and screeches that emit from inside the house.

8. Supply each lucky guest with a paper towel to dry their hands as they come out of the house.

#32 The President's Dog

Ages 6 and up
2 or more players, the more the better
No supplies necessary

This is good traveling game or great when sitting around a campfire. It is a challenging word game, and it keeps players focused on the order of the alphabet.

1. Everyone thinks of an adjective to describe the President's dog beginning with the letter "A." For example, "The President's dog is an amazing dog." Each takes a turn with the letter "A."

2. Next, everyone takes a turn thinking up an adjective beginning with the letter "B." "The President's dog is a brave dog." And so on through the alphabet.

#33 Dance of the Seven Veils

Ages 4 and up.
2–6 players
You'll need:

- different colored scarves for each child and/or pieces of tulle or chiffon-like fabric you can find inexpensively at a fabric store
- dance music such as the music from *Fantasia; Coppelia* by Leo Delibes; "Flight of the Bumble Bee" by Nikolai Rimsky-Korsakov; *An American in Paris* by George Gershwin. Check these out at your local library
- enough space for kids to stretch out their arms and twirl around

Kids love to dance and are naturally good at it. You can help them express themselves creatively by adding interesting music and scarves to the experience.

1. Have children wear comfortable clothing. Their feet should be bare.

2. Let each child pick out a scarf or two. Start the music and watch them discover movement with the scarves.

3. It's helpful to play a piece of music several times so that the kids become familiar with it and can anticipate certain passages and move in response to them.

#34 Homemade Aviation

Ages 6–8
1–4 players
You'll need:

- sheets of paper (8½ x 11 inches)
- markers or stickers to decorate plane (optional)

Remember making paper jet planes and trying for hours to get that long trajectory? Here's a simple, tried-and-true design that will send kids off into the blue beyond!

1. Fold the sheet of paper in half lengthwise. Crease the fold firmly.

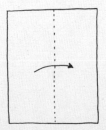

2. Fold the bottom corners to the center and crease hard.

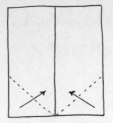

3. Fold each of the flaps in half again. The new flaps should meet in the center. The point should be sharp.

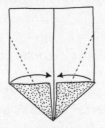

4. Fold the flaps again, so they meet at the center line.

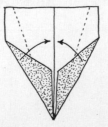

5. Fold the jet in half lengthwise, folding sides down and away from you.

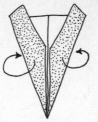

6. Spread the wings, and hold the base of the aircraft with your thumb and forefinger. Now the plane is ready for takeoff. Fasten your seat belts, sit back, and enjoy the ride!

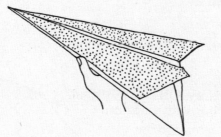

#35 Valentines for Lunch

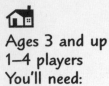

Ages 3 and up
1–4 players
You'll need:

- sandwich bread
- raspberry jelly
- chocolate syrup
- a large heart-shaped cookie cutter

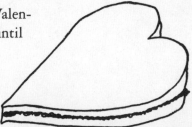

This is a great activity for Valentine's Day, but why wait until then to have kids make these sweet heart sandwiches for lunch?

1. Make sandwiches with the jelly and syrup.

2. Place cookie cutter on top of each sandwich and push down firmly to stamp out the heart-shaped sandwich.

3. Arrange on a colorful plate and serve. These tasty sandwiches are good with milk or raspberry-cranberry juice.

#36 Read Between the Lines

Ages 8 and up
Any number of players
You'll need:

- onionskin paper or regular bond paper (available in stationery stores)
- a ballpoint pen
- a small cup of lemon juice (fresh or from a bottle)
- a calligraphy pen with a broad nib (the inexpensive kind you can find in an arts and crafts store)

This activity explains where the popular saying "Read between the lines" comes from. In the 18th and 19th centuries, secret messages were communicated by writing with lemon juice between the lines of a letter written with ink.

1. Ask the child to think about secret and mysterious things to write about, such as where she hid a treasure or the recipe for

a magical potion or a secret code (words spelled backward, or numbers representing letters of the alphabet).

2. The child then writes a simple letter to a friend or a family member with a ballpoint pen, leaving enough room between the lines for the secret message.

3. She dips the pen nib into the lemon juice and writes her secret message between the lines written in ink.

4. When the lemon juice is dry, hold the letter up to a lamp or lit candle to read the secret message.

5. Roll up the letter, tie it with a ribbon, and give or mail it to the intended recipient with instructions on how to "read between the lines."

#37 Silly Faces

Ages 4 and up
Any number of players
You'll need:

- black eyebrow pencil or black crayon that's easily removable
- an old lipstick
- baby wipes (to remove makeup)
- a bed

In this game, kids get to experiment with face parts and makeup. It's fun for the kids, and if it's an adult and child, the child can create a new face for the adult.

1. The child lies on his back on a bed, his head hanging upside down over the side.

2. The other child draws a face with the eyes on either side of the real mouth, paints a mouth on the forehead, and draws little pink or red circles for cheeks.

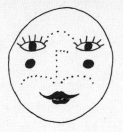

3. The child whose face has been "painted" closes his eyes and wiggles his face to make funny expressions.

4. The other child can hold up a mirror so the painted child can see his new face!

5. The children trade places so everyone gets a new face!

#38 It's All a Shell Game

Ages 4–8
2 players
You'll need:

- 3 medium-sized clamshells, as identical as possible (about 2½ inches across) or small paper cups if shells are not available
- a dried bean or a pea

This is an ancient game using shells that still entertains today.

1. Place shells on a table or any surface that won't scratch. You can start the game for the child. Hide the bean or pea under one of the shells; line them up in a row and slowly move the shells around so that they end up in different places but are still in a row. Stop, and ask the child if he can point to the shell hiding the bean or pea.

2. Do this a few more times, then switch so that the child gets to be the trickster. Kids love to play this game with each other. You can make it more competitive by throwing in a prize (e.g., the person who guesses correctly three times wins a sticker of some kind).

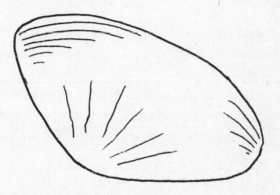

#39 How Does Your Garden Grow?

🌳🌷🌱

Ages 4 and up
Any number of players
You'll need:

- the following plant seeds: sunflower, hollyhock (dwarf), Johnny-jump-up, lamb's ears, basil, mint, and nasturtium
- a patch of soil that gets moderate to full sun
- a trowel
- a fine-spray nozzle for the hose

If you're fortunate enough to have a garden, why not put a little area aside for children? Their garden should be a manageable little plot for them to sink their toes and hands into. Starting a garden with seeds cultivates patience and offers a sense of the cycle of life. If you can't find the seeds for these plants in the stores, you can substitute seedlings or small plants. To explore gardening with kids even further, a good book on the subject is *Kids Garden* by Avery Hart and Paul Mantell (Williamson Publishing).

Discuss ahead of time what sorts of plants and flowers and herbs the children would like to grow, and help draw a simple plan to show where the seeds are to go. Buy the seeds from a reliable garden store and check the packets for expiration dates. Here's a simple design for a flower and herb garden:

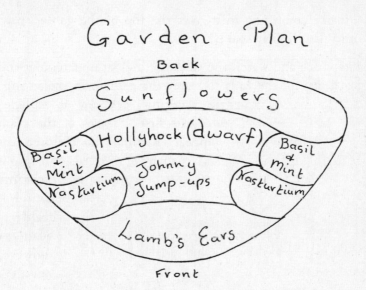

Garden Plan

Back

Sunflowers

Hollyhock (dwarf)

Basil + Mint

Nasturtium

Johnny Jump-ups

Basil + Mint

Nasturtium

Lamb's Ears

Front

1. Kids dig up the soil with a hand trowel so that the soil is loose and airy. Smooth out the soil so that it's fairly flat and even.

2. Dampen the soil with a fine spray.

3. Plant seeds according to their needs—for example, sunflower seeds need to be an inch down into the soil. Check seed packets for instructions. Sprinkle a thin layer of sand or soil over the top of the very tiny seeds.

4. Finally, spray fine mist over the top of the garden patch until it is lightly soaked.

5. Step back and watch the garden grow. Set up a regular time each day for the kids to water the garden. In the spring a gentle watering each day is sufficient until the first 2 leaves of the plants appear. Remind the children that many of the seeds will sprout and grow into beautiful healthy plants; however, not all will, and this is just a normal part of life.

#40 The Grass Is Always Greener

Ages 4 and up
Any number of players
You'll need:

- clay pots or a small window box
- potting soil
- grass seed—you can buy just a cup of seed from a good garden supply store

For a simple indoor garden in the colder days of spring, grow a patch of fresh grass in clay pots or a window box in a sunny window. Kids love to watch the first blades of green push up from the soil.

1. The child fills pots or box with soil to an inch from the top.

2. Sprinkle seeds over the top of the soil, making a blanket of seeds.

3. Place in a sunny window.

4. Water gently each day.

5. When the grass reaches 3 or 4 inches, the child can trim it with small scissors, even shaping it to create waves of grass.

#41 A Doll's Birthday

Ages 3–6
2–4 players
You'll need:

- inexpensive wrapping paper
- scissors
- tape
- construction paper or white paper (8½ x 11 inches)
- crayons
- glitter glue for cards
- un-iced cupcakes, one for each child
- ready-made icing in a can
- small colored candies
- sprinkles
- birthday candles

Birthdays can be celebrated anytime of the year. Why not create a pretend birthday party for a special doll or stuffed animal? Children love the idea of celebrations and become engaged with all the details of wrapping gifts, making birthday cards, and decorating cupcakes.

1. The child places the birthday doll or stuffed animal in a special chair or on a table for display. Kids can gather up any

toys that they'd like to wrap and use as presents for the doll or animal. Help them cut the paper and wrap the toys if necessary.

2. Cards can be made by folding the sheets of paper in half or cutting them to any size. Children can write HAPPY BIRTHDAY or draw any picture of choice, using markers, crayons, and glitter glue.

3. Each child coats the top of a cupcake with icing, decorates it with the colored candy and sprinkles, and finally adds a candle to complete the "birthday cake."

4. The children can display the presents and "birthday cakes" on a table near the doll or animal. You can help with lighting the candles. They then all sing "Happy Birthday," and "help" the doll blow out the candles on the cakes. The best part is when they get to eat their own personal cupcake.

#42 The Corner Grocery Store

Ages 4 and up
2–4 players
You'll need:

- bag of flour
- cereal
- bag of sugar
- pasta
- coffee
- cans of soup
- cookies
- rice
- juice
- toilet paper
- soda
- paper towels
- sponges
- a bell
- a shoe box for the "register"
- paper and markers to make signs and price tags

(You can use toy food items, but the real thing is much more fun!)

Kids love to set up shop and practice the age-old art of commerce. In this activity they make a mock grocery store from items found in the kitchen. You can use play money, make your own money from paper and tinfoil, or give them pennies, nickels, and dimes to add an element of reality to the game.

1. The grocery store owner wears an apron to distinguish him from the customers.

2. Kids write little price tags to put next to the merchandise. Flour is 5 cents; pasta is 10 cents; etc.

3. Set all the goods on a table or kitchen counter, and arrange them so that they are easily seen by the customers.

4. As a customer comes into the "store," he rings a bell that sits on the counter near the register (a shoe box).

5. The owner greets the customer and asks him what he would like today.

6. Everyone gets a turn to be the owner. Customers must restock the store after they've done their shopping.

#43 Abracadabra Magic Wand

Ages 4–6
Any number of players
You'll need:

- newspaper for the wand
- aluminum foil or gold foil
- colored tissue or crepe paper
- clear tape
- white glue
- cardboard
- markers
- glitter
- scissors

When kids are in the mood for some magic, show them how to make a magic wand. It's as easy as a nose wiggle.

1. Roll 2 sheets of newspaper tightly together, widthwise, and tape to make the wand.

2. Cover the wand with foil, and tape it securely.

3. Cut 2 star shapes from the cardboard.

4. Cut long strips of colored tissue or crepe paper for the streamers.

5. Using markers, color the stars and decorate them with glitter, then let them dry. Glue streamers to the top of the wand and let them dry. Glue the 2 star shapes on either side of the top of the wand. You may need to secure them with tape as well. Now the kids are ready for some "Bibbity Bobbity Boo!"

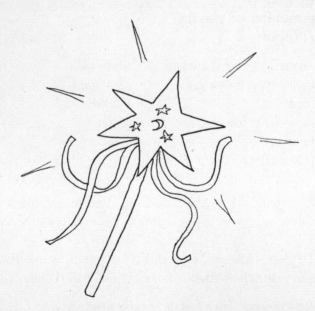

#44 Flower Power

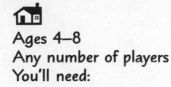

Ages 4–8
Any number of players
You'll need:

- several white flowers (carnations are fine)
- the top of a celery stalk
- several drinking glasses filled halfway with water
- vials of food coloring
- scissors

Watch flowers change color before your eyes. This pretty science experiment shows how water travels up stems to nourish all the plant cells.

1. Cut long stems of carnations and celery to about 8 inches or less.

2. In each glass put 10 drops of a different food coloring.

3. Put a flower or celery stalk in each glass.

4. Watch how the flowers and celery change color.

For an interesting variation, split a carnation stem by slicing carefully lengthwise to the top of the flower, and put each half of the stem in a different color of water. Each half of the flower will be a different color.

#45 To Float or Sink

Ages 6–10
Any number of players
You'll need:

- a small glass tank or bowl of water
- a piece of modeling clay rolled into a 2-inch ball
- several marbles

Oh, a sailor's life for me! This experiment is probably not what pirates in the old days thought about, but this is a fun and easy way for kids to understand how things float.

1. Drop the marbles and clay ball into the water and watch them sink.

2. Now take them out and shape the clay into a small bowl with a hollowed out space in the middle. Place this on the water. It floats.

3. Now place some "cargo" in your "boat" and watch it sink a little but still stay afloat.

Because you've created more surface area with the clay by shaping it into a bowl, it has displaced or pushed more water out of the way, allowing it to receive a stronger upward push from the water underneath. That's how big cargo ships at sea can stay afloat!

#46 Penny Pitching

Ages 8 and up
2 or more players
You'll need:

- 10 pennies per player
- a flat surface near a wall
- chalk or colored tape

Children get to test their aim and concentration with this fun coin-toss game.

1. Mark 2 6-foot lines out from the wall, about 4 feet apart. Mark another line at the 6-foot mark, parallel to the wall.

2. The first player stands behind the pitching line and throws a penny against the wall.

3. The second player does the same, and tries to hit the first player's penny. If he succeeds, he takes both pennies and gets to pitch the next penny.

4. Players take turns until someone ends up with all the pennies.

5. Some variations are: (1) pitching one's penny as close to the wall as possible and (2) if a player's penny falls within a certain distance from the opponent's penny, he wins.

#47 Eat More Sprouts!

🏠

Ages 4–8
Any number of players
You'll need:

- a selection of sprout seeds (e.g., mung, alfalfa, sunflower) from a health food store
- a large Mason jar
- coarse nylon mesh 6 inches square
- a heavy rubber band

Kids get to grow their own food! This project helps children appreciate how food is grown, and they get to reap what they sow.

1. Place 1 tablespoon of mixed seeds into the Mason jar. Place mesh over the top and secure it with a rubber band.

2. Pour fresh clean water into the jar through the mesh and swirl it around, rinsing the seeds. Pour the water out and let the jar stand upside down to drain.

3. Place the jar in bright light but not direct sun. Each day around the same time, rinse the seeds, thereby watering them at the same time. In 1–2 days, they'll start to sprout.

4. When the sprouts are about 1–2 inches long, they're ready to harvest. Let the child pick out her favorite dressing and toss the sprouts with other fresh greens, or serve them just as they are. Bon appetit!

48 Stained Glass Fantasia

Ages 4–8
Any number of players
You'll need:

- different colors of tissue paper
- heavy construction paper for border, any color
- a roll of waxed paper
- glue stick
- scissors
- an iron

This is a cheery rainy day project that requires just a few materials. Kids make stained glass panels that hang in windows and brighten up their rooms.

1. The child tears off a piece of waxed paper small enough to fit inside her bedroom window.

2. After choosing colors from the tissue paper to place inside panel, she tears out different sized shapes and arranges them

on the waxed paper panel. Secure each shape to the waxed paper with a little glue. When the design is ready, the adult can help by ironing the back of the waxed paper panel, placing brown paper between iron and panel, and pressing gently until the tissue sticks to the waxed paper.

3. Glue or tape strips of the heavy construction paper around edges of waxed paper for the frame.

4. Hang the panel in a bright window so that light can shine through the colored "glass."

#49 Hot Potato

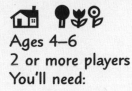

Ages 4–6
2 or more players
You'll need:

- a real potato (for the traditionalists)
- a beanbag or small stuffed animal is fine

This is a good standby favorite that is great for a party game or can be played anytime, indoors or out.

1. Children form a circle, standing.

2. The "hot potato" is passed from player to player as quickly as possible. Anyone who drops the "potato" is out.

3. The last player wins.

4. A variation is to use music. When the music stops, the person holding the "potato" is out.

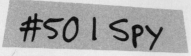

#50 I Spy

Ages 4–6
Any number of players
No supplies necessary

Though you can play this game anywhere, it is fine when traveling or going on a walk. It also heightens observation skills.

1. The first child chooses an object, color, or shape, and gives her clue: "I spy with my little eye, something (or color, or shape) that begins with the letter _____."

2. The other kids take turns guessing what the object, color, or shape might be.

3. The first player to guess correctly chooses the next object.

#51 Stiltskins

Ages 6 and up
Any number of players
You'll need:

- 2 coffee cans per child
- jute or propylene twine

You may have done this as a kid: walking on coffee cans that are strapped to your feet, and suddenly feeling a little more grown-up. It's fun to watch kids do this for the first time. This is best done outside, where there are fewer obstacles.

1. Drill or punch 2 holes an inch from the bottom on either side of 1 can.

2. Cut 4 pieces of twine, 2 yards each.

3. Tie the 2 cut ends of the same piece together, to double it up for strength. Thread it through a hole from the inside of the can, pulling it all the way through until the knot blocks the hole. Repeat on the other side. Now rig the other can in the same way.

4. Have the child stand on top of both cans, feet positioned evenly over the cans. The adult can assist by tying the string over the feet as if tying shoelaces. Make sure the fit is snug.

5. Now child is ready to stilt-walk. Be ready to steady her if she loses balance. In no time at all she'll be a pro, and will want to run away and join the circus!

Story Time

Reading to children is fundamental in establishing bonds and in developing good reading skills. Reading to kids anytime—indoors and out—is great. It's also important to establish a story time routine each day. For many families, this usually happens at bedtime, since reading to children often helps them to fall asleep (although I've known many an adult who has succumbed to the Sandman while reading to a child).

Here are some suggestions for good reading. This list is a selection of titles taken from *The New York Times Parent's Guide to the Best Books for Children*, by Eden Lipson and Susan Luke. Even though reference is made to age groups, children's levels of appreciation vary, so feel free to try them out on older and younger children.

Preschoolers to 1st-graders

Angry Arthur by Hiawyn Oram (Sunburst Books)

Cloudy with a Chance of Meatballs by Judith Barrett (Aladdin Paperbacks)

The Emperor's New Clothes by Hans Christian Andersen, illustrated by Anne Rockwell (Houghton Mifflin)

Goodnight, Moon by Margaret Wise Brown (HarperCollins)

Millions of Cats by Wanda Gag (Paper Star)

Up to 2nd-graders

The Fool of the World and the Flying Ship by Arthur Ransome (Farrar Straus & Giroux)

The Giving Tree by Shel Silverstein (HarperCollins)

In the Night Kitchen by Maurice Sendak (HarperCollins)

The Little Red Lighthouse and the Great Gray Bridge by Hildegard Swift (Harcourt Brace)

The Red Balloon by Albert Lamorisse (Doubleday)

When We Were Very Young by A. A. Milne (Puffin)

For a wide range of ages:

The Adventures of Pinocchio by Carlo Collodi (Dover Publications)

The Borrowers by Mary Norton (Harcourt Brace)

Charlotte's Web by E. B. White (HarperCollins)

Mary Poppins, revised edition, by P. L. Travers (Harcourt Brace)
The Tales of Uncle Remus: The Adventures of Brer Rabbit by Joel Chandler Harris (Puffin)
Zlateh the Goat and Other Stories by Isaac Bashevis Singer (HarperCollins)

Grab Bag

Here are a few handy ideas that will do in a pinch.

Gobstopper

Stop the presses! This game has to be one of the best travel games I've experienced. No more "Mom, I'm bored" noises from the backseat. It's best for ages 6 and up, and for 2 or more players.

Before you load the crew into the car, get enough jawbreakers, one for every child—the bigger the better. The ones that change color are even more fun. Save this game for last, after you've exhausted all others and you're craving some quiet time.

Hand a jawbreaker to each child, and tell them the child with the last surviving jawbreaker wins the game.

Moving Tales

A very simple and quick way to keep a child entertained while traveling in car, train, or plane is to supply a tape player with headphones and a favorite book on tape. This activity is especially good when more active games are played out and quiet time is called for.

Spinning Stars

If you find yourself in an open field or park with soft grass, here's an easy game to play. Kids have been doing this by themselves since the beginning of time. You can join in. It works best for ages 3 and up, and is great for 2 or more players.

Children stand and stretch their arms out straight to the side. Make sure there's enough room between them. Have them slowly start to turn in circles. Slowly increase their speed. Tell them to go as fast as they like. When they are dizzy, they can fall on the soft grass. As they look up around them, the world and all the stars will still be spinning.

Kiss!!!! Kiss!!!!

This is a lovely bonding game for a child aged 3–6 and makes the child feel very special, since she gets all the one-on-one attention. All you need is a few chocolate kisses.

At a distance from the child—across the room, or from the front seat of the car to the backseat, say: "I'm going to blow you a kiss. Are you ready?" Get her to catch it on her cheek. Have her send you one back. You, too, can catch it on the cheek. You can also pretend to be blown over by it, holding your cheek as you catch it. (This always gets a big laugh.) Do this a few times, moving farther away each time. (In the car you can keep the same distance.) You will soon be blowing "long-distance" kisses. For the grand finale, when it's your turn, hold out a chocolate in your hand as the final KISS! She can run to you and get her chocolate kiss. This will be one of her favorite games to play!

About the Author

Photo credit: Peter Pearce

In the early 1980s Ellen van Wees studied early childhood development in her native Australia. She lived in the Netherlands and Italy before relocating to the United States, where she began a children's party entertainment business, which she has had for over 10 years. For 15 years she has been a professional puppeteer, and along with teaching puppetry in the New York City schools, she designs and builds experimental puppet pieces for adult audiences.